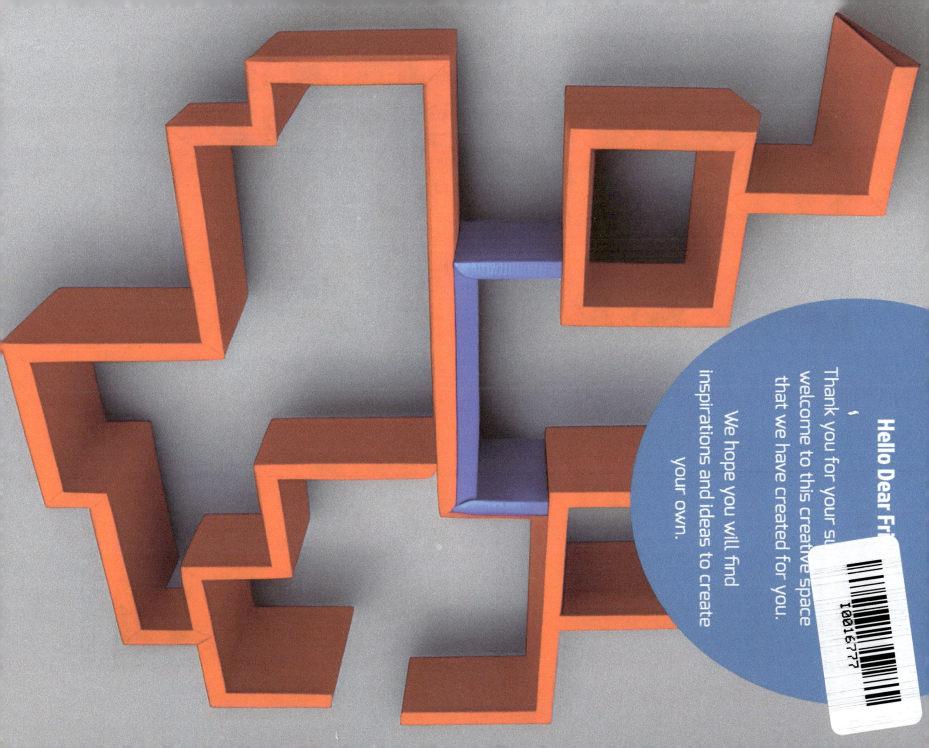

TABLE OF CONTENT

CREATURES P. 4-75

DECOR P. 140-213

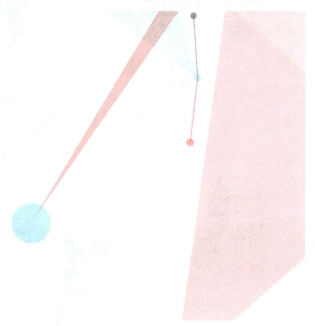

INTRO P. 1-3,   END P, 214-216

ABSTRACTS P. 76 -139

There is no wrong way to use this book.

Following on the success of our first two collections, here is the biggest collection we've created. You will find a wide range of project images. These will expand your already stretched imagination. Use at your own risk!!

Here are more suggestions on how to use this book:

- use one images to create challenges on social media
- print / cut up to make greeting cards or post cards
- have a 'tell me what you see' party with friends
- create your own pattern based on image and sell on ETSY
- offer a class and show people how to make them
- print / glue images on a plain journal to make your own
- is perfect gift to any artsy friend
- take notes of the color combinations for your own projects
- get inspired and procreate these in your own way!

Ready? Let's go!

4

CREATURES

70

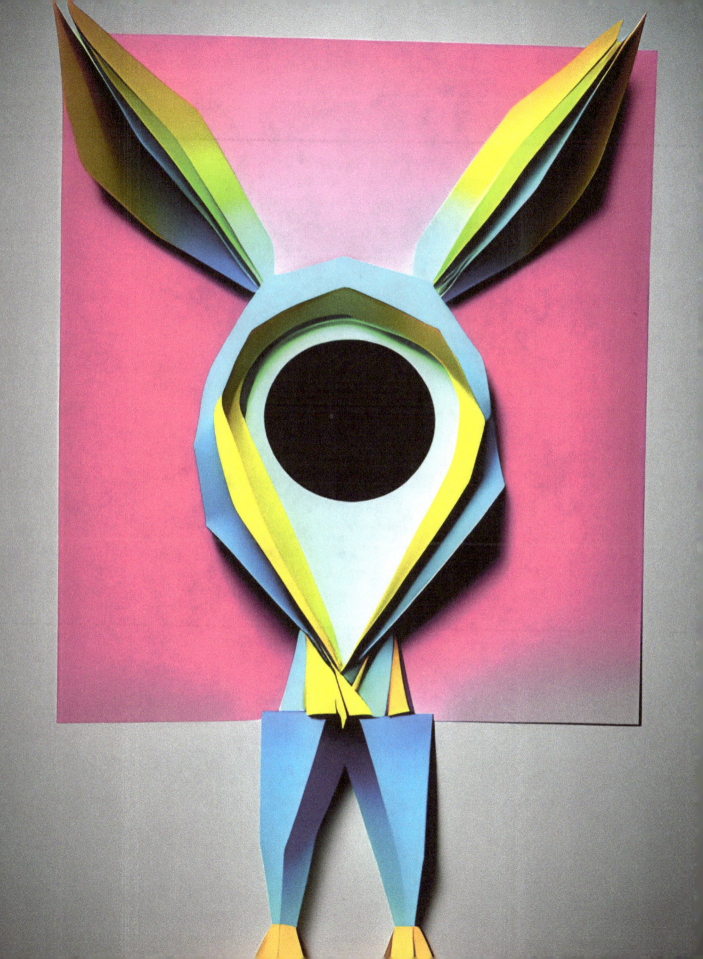

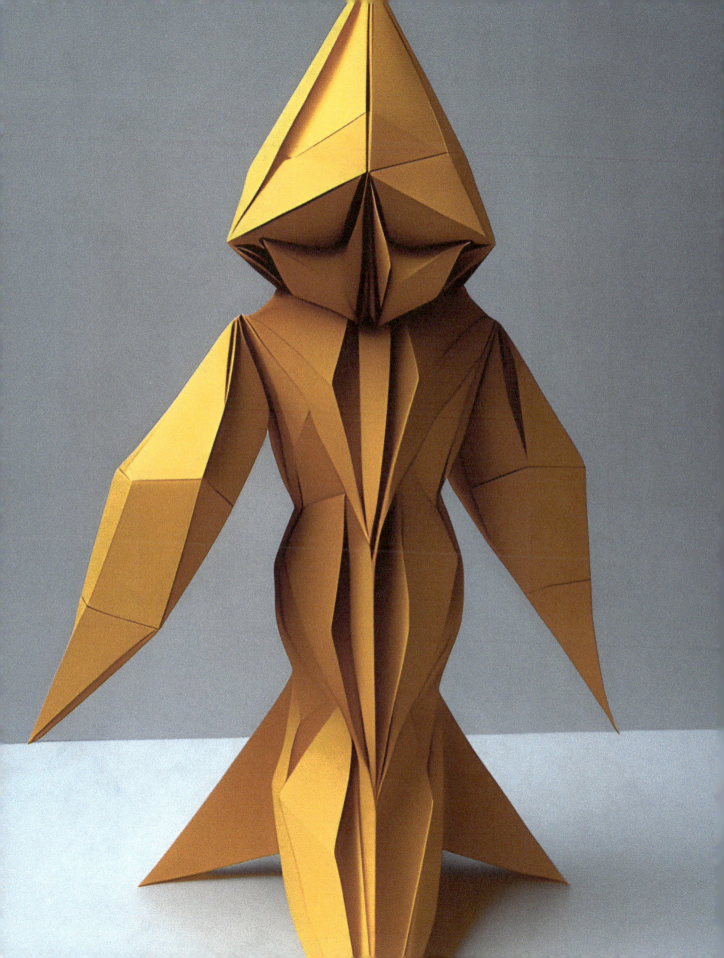

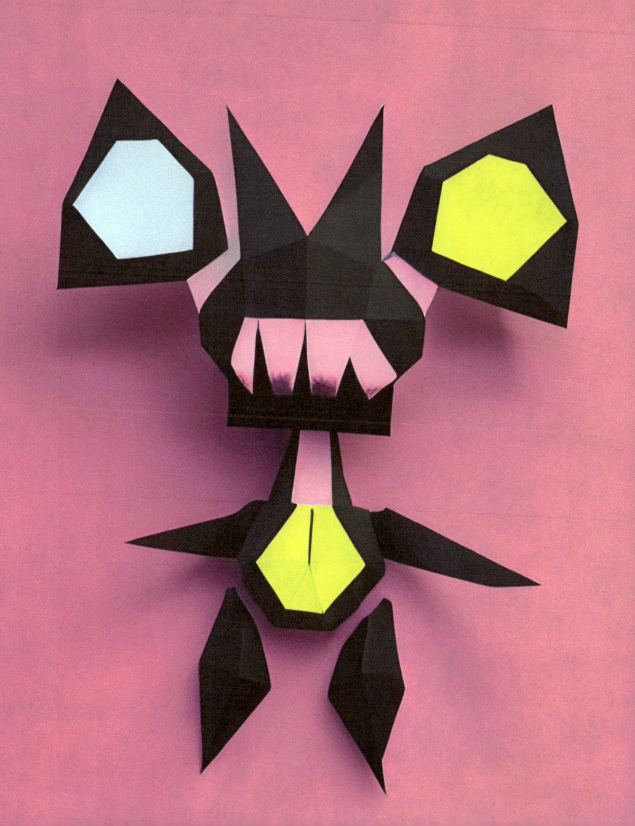

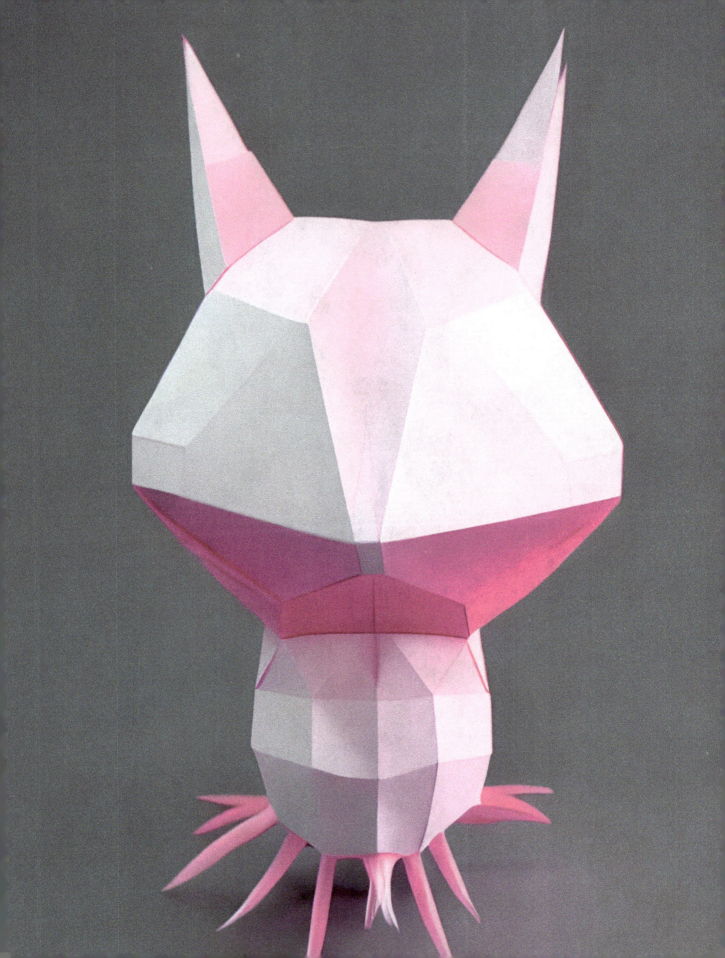

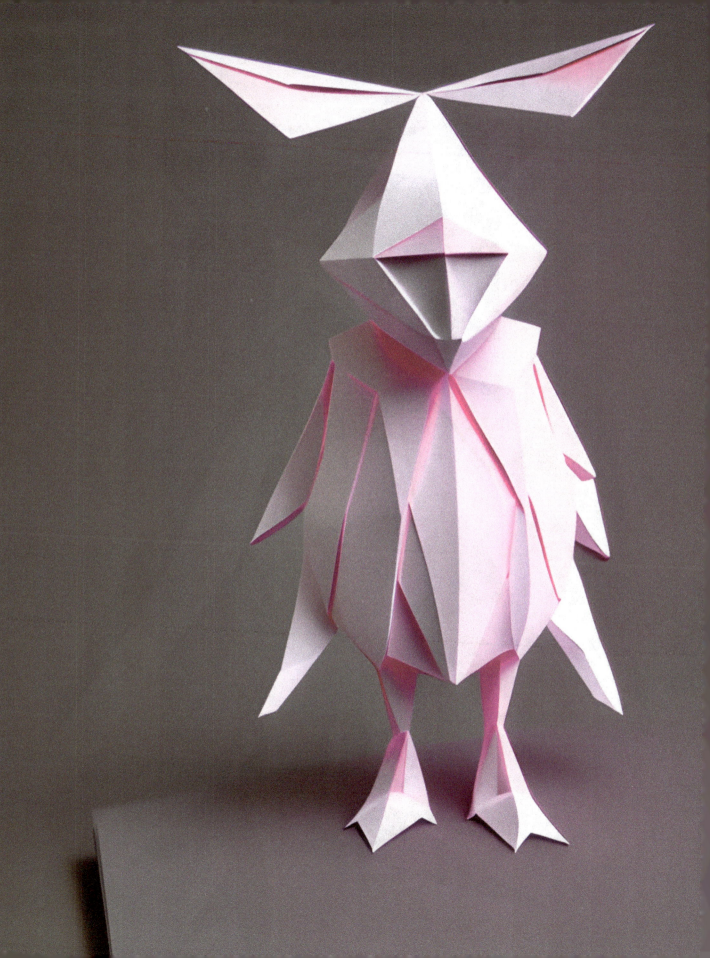

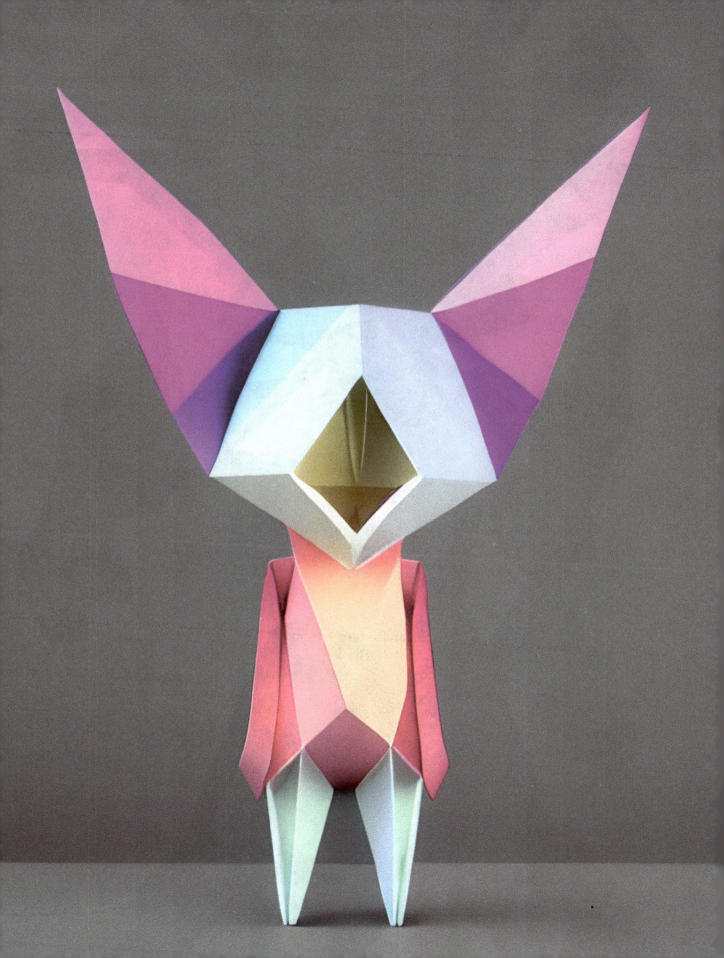

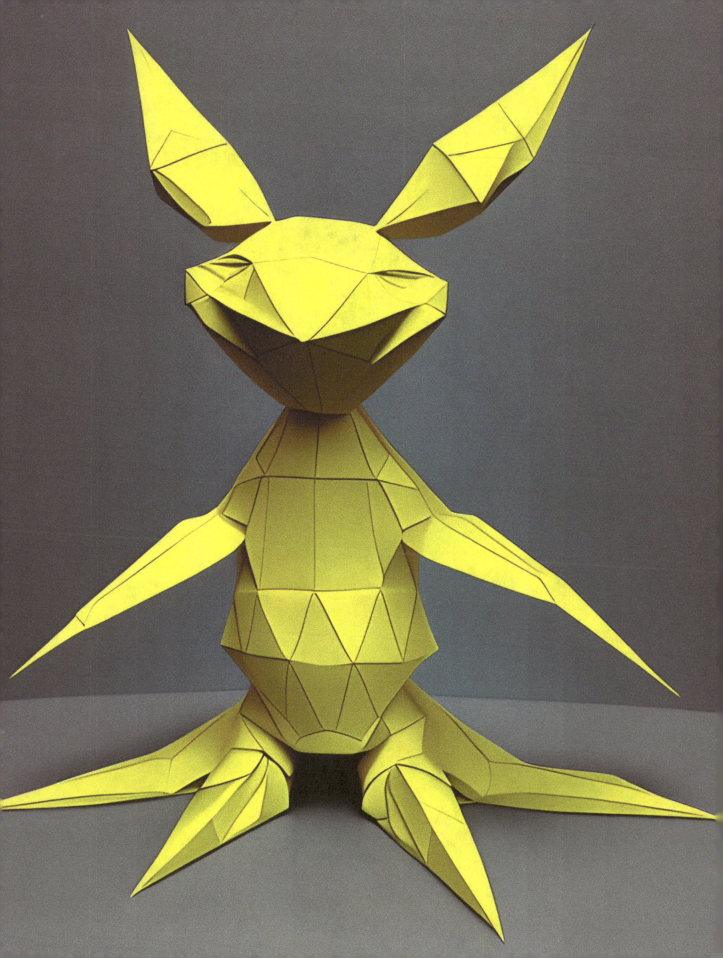

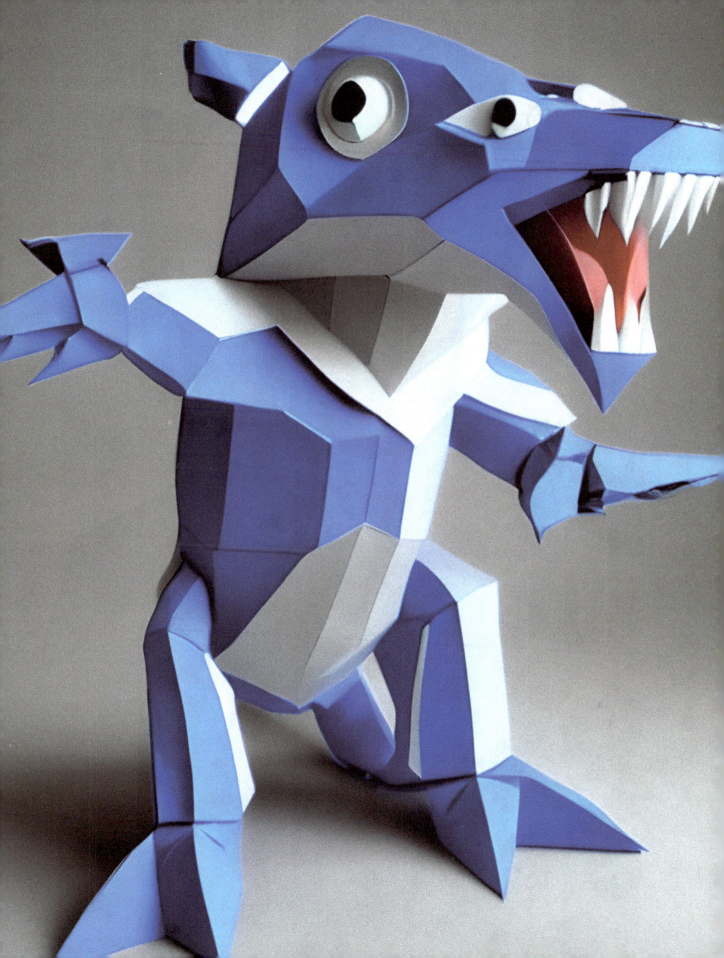

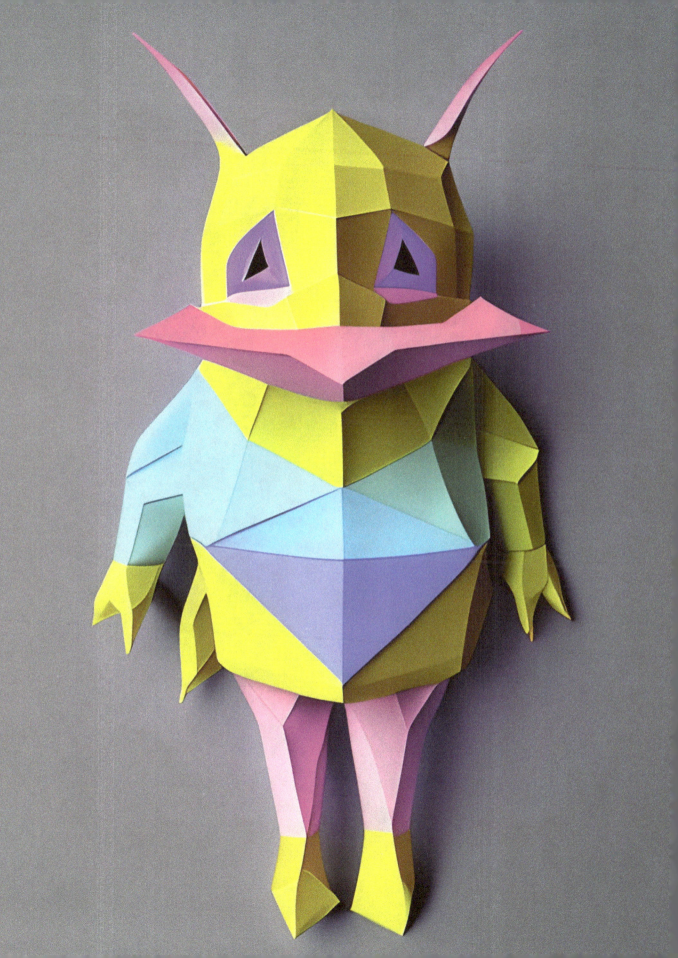

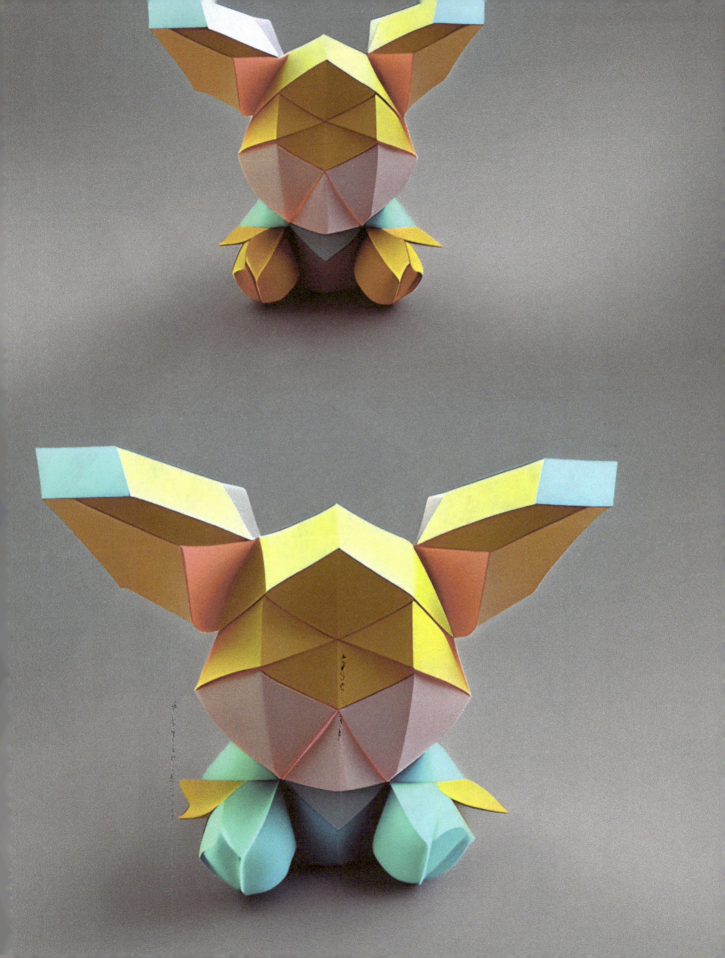

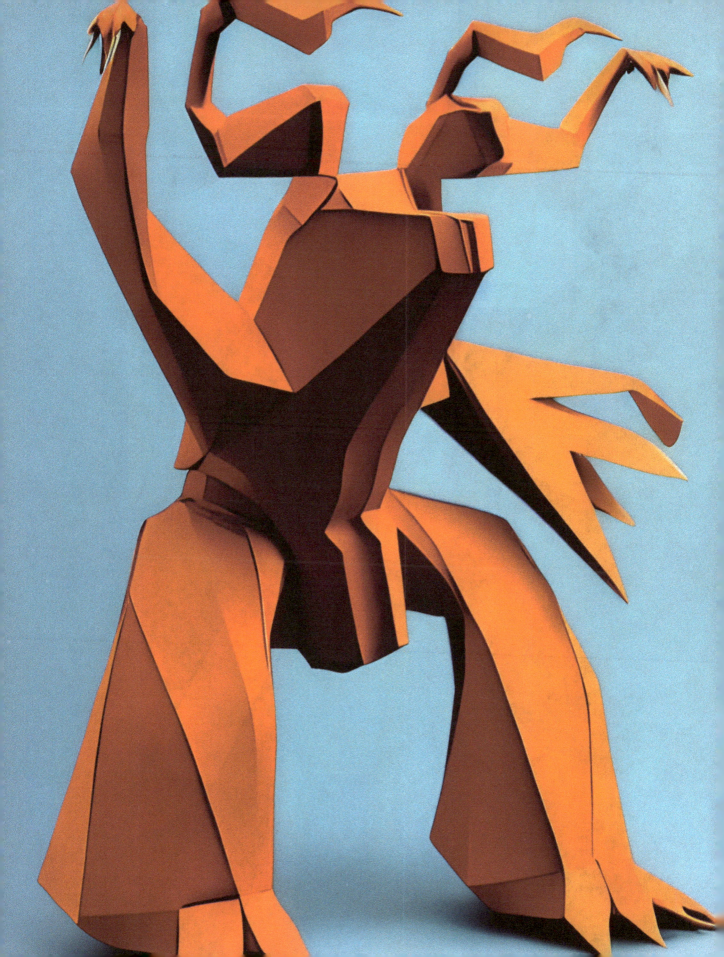

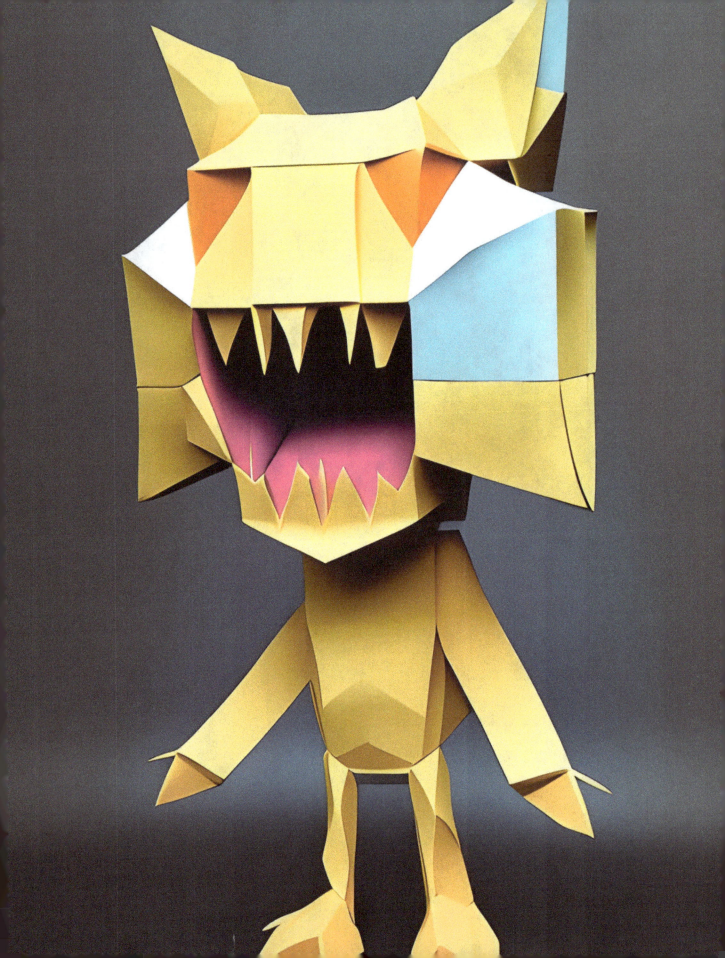

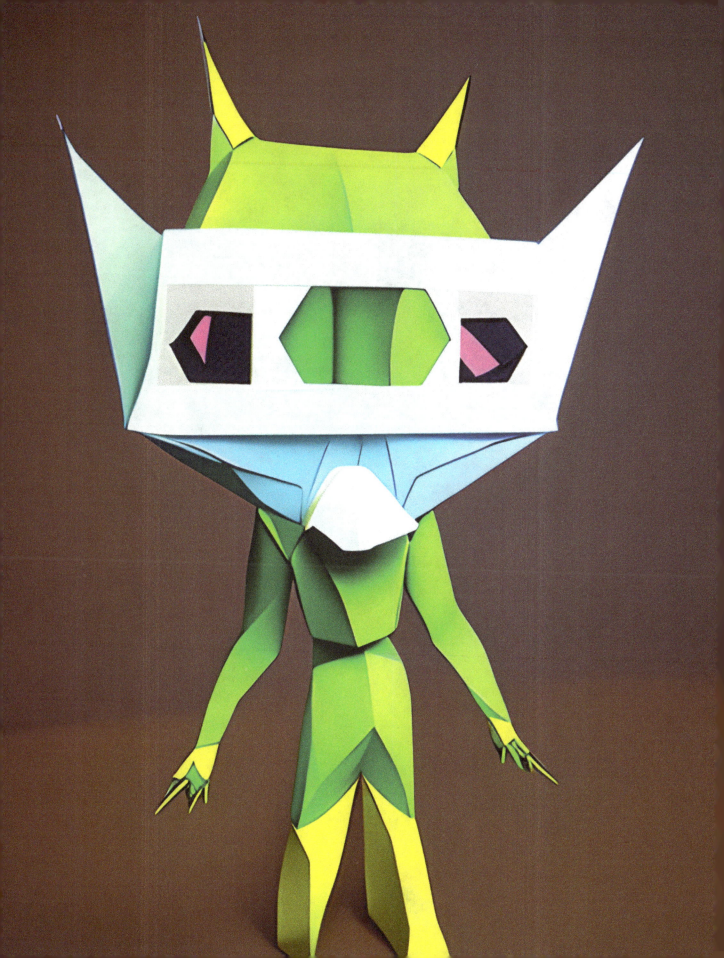

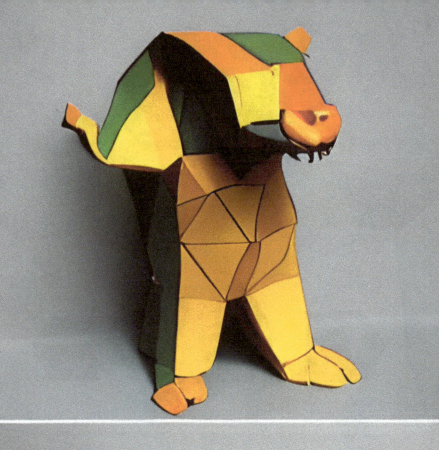

ABSTRACTS

64

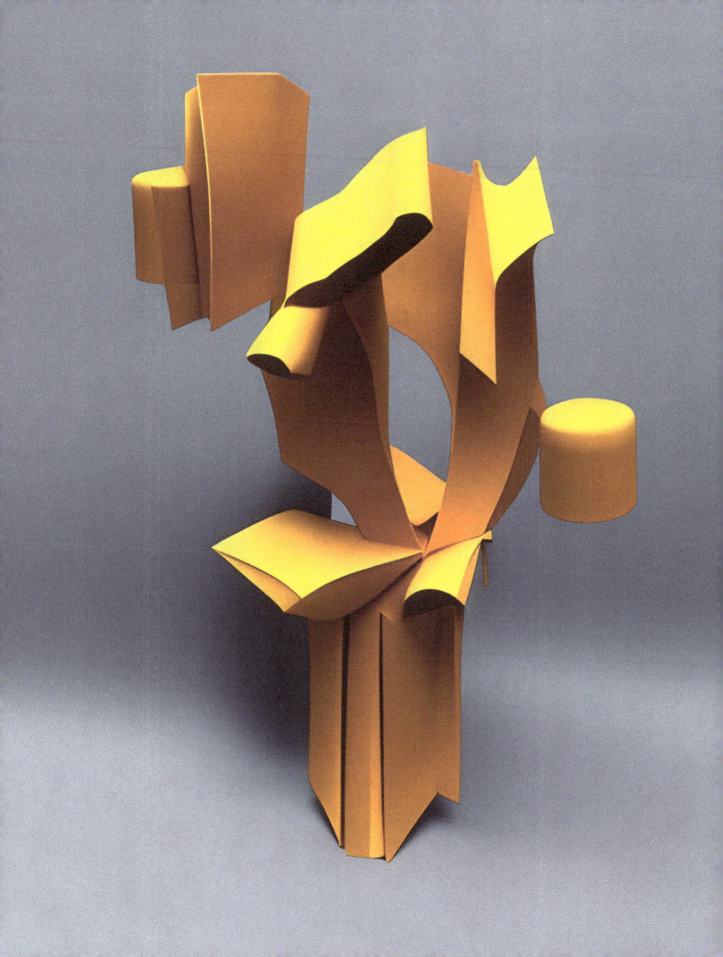

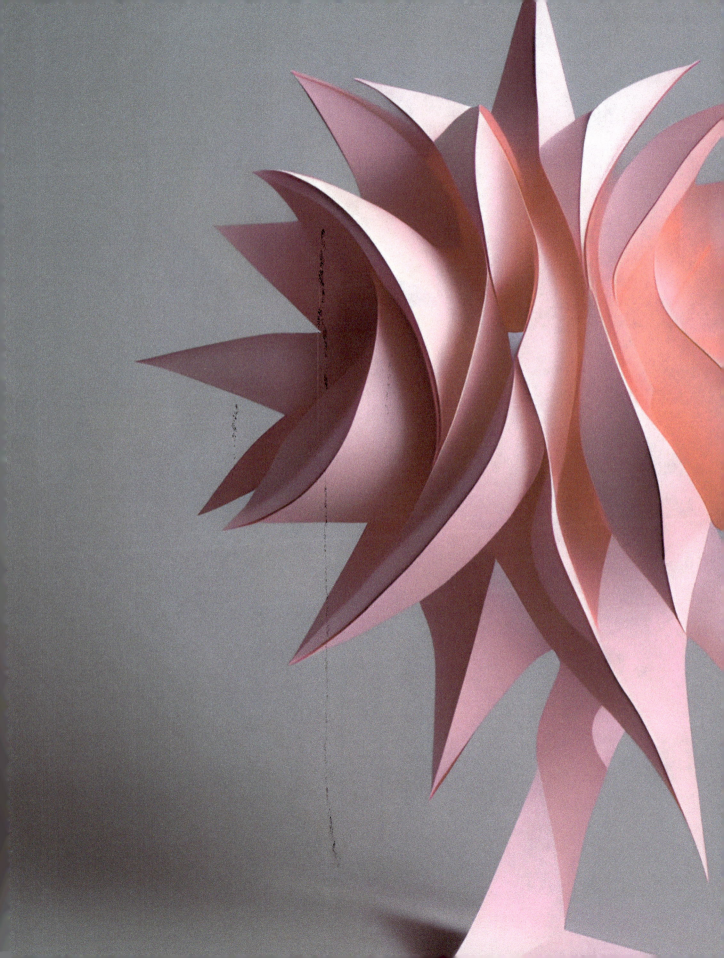

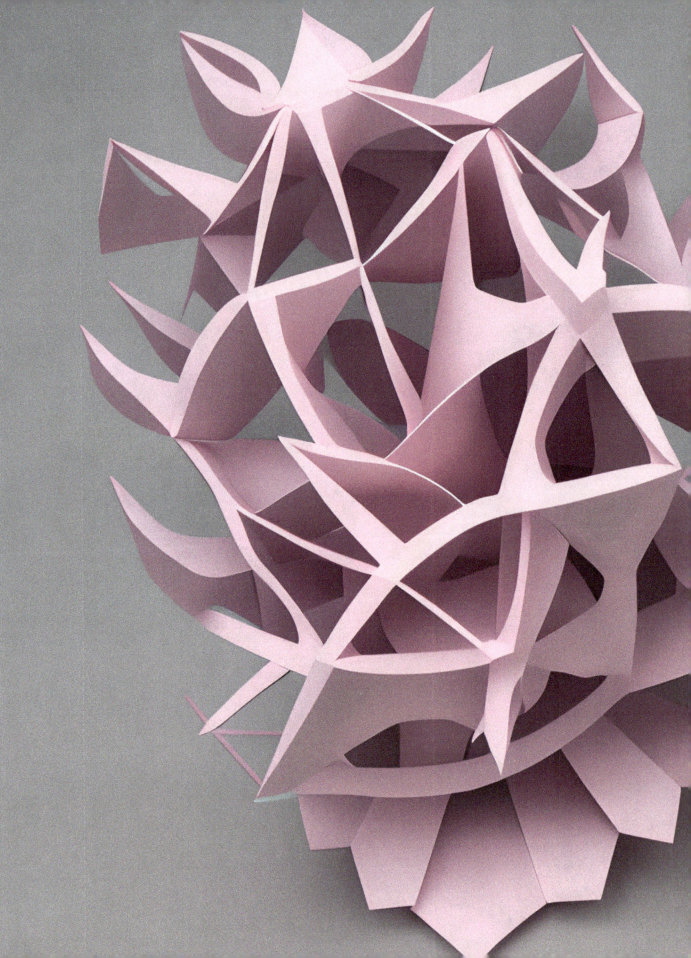

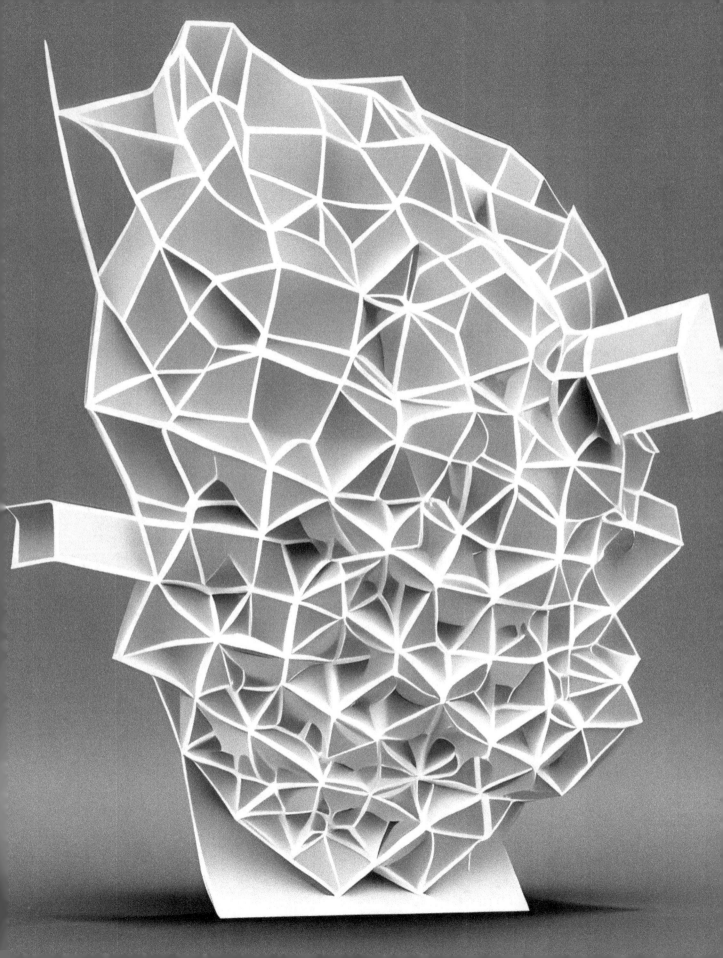

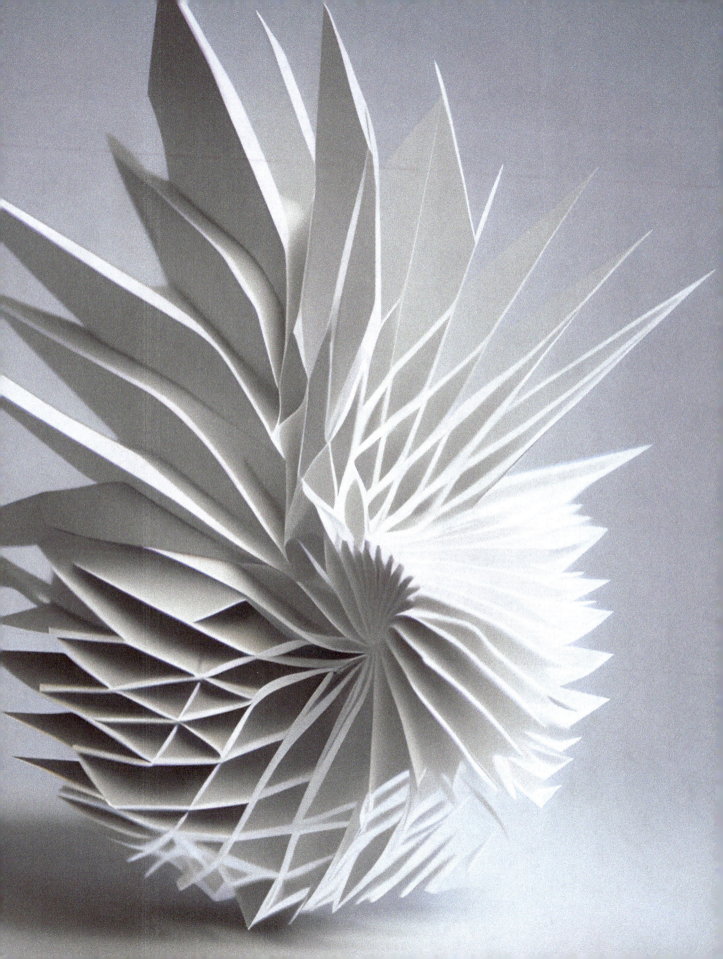

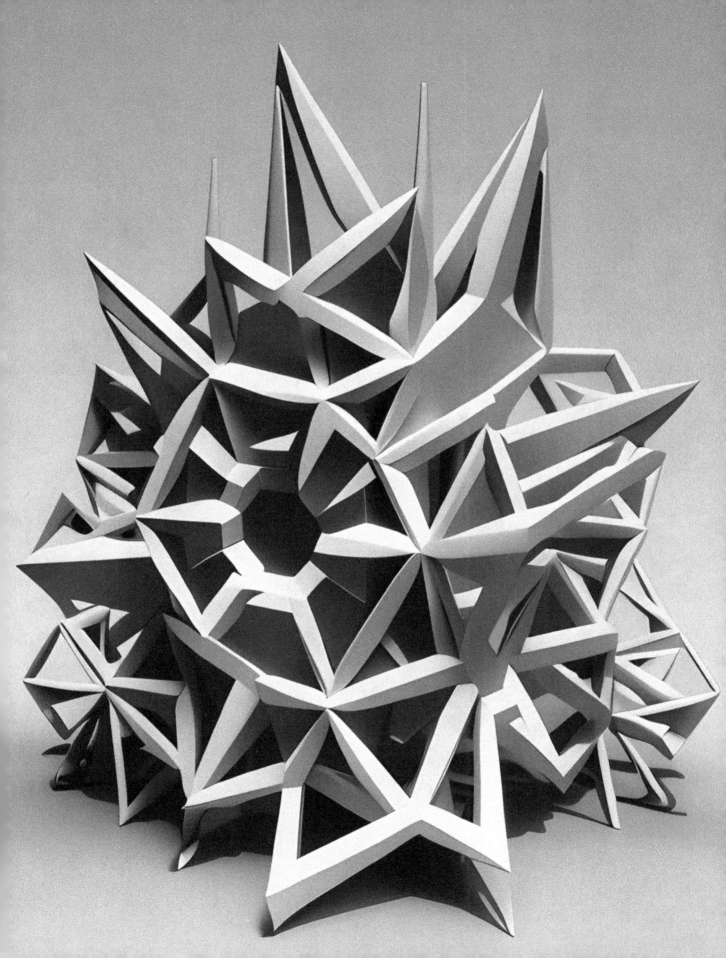

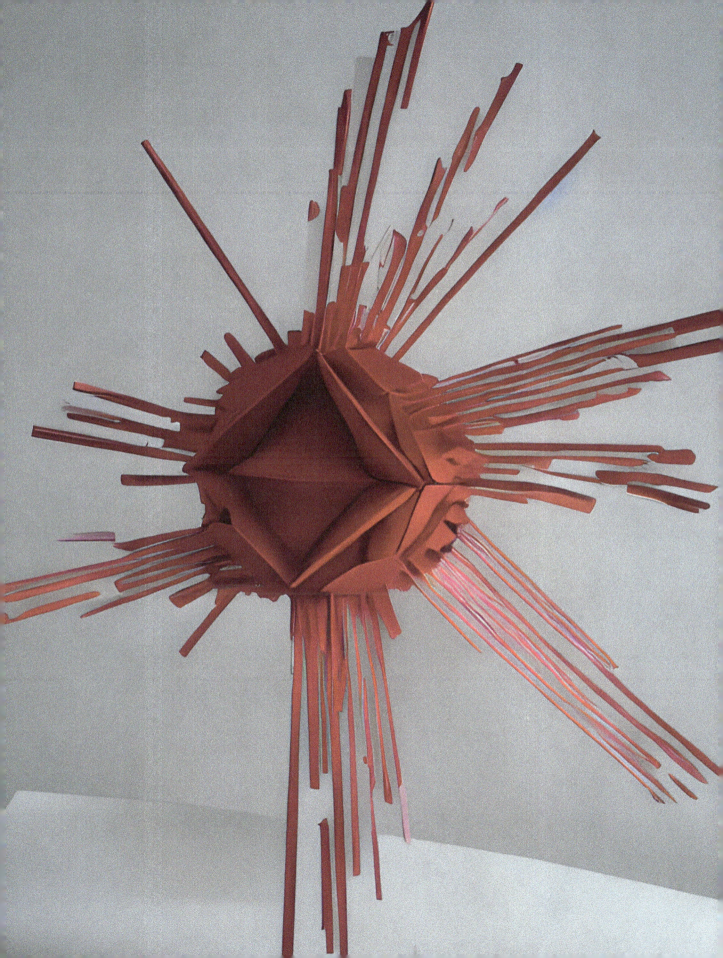

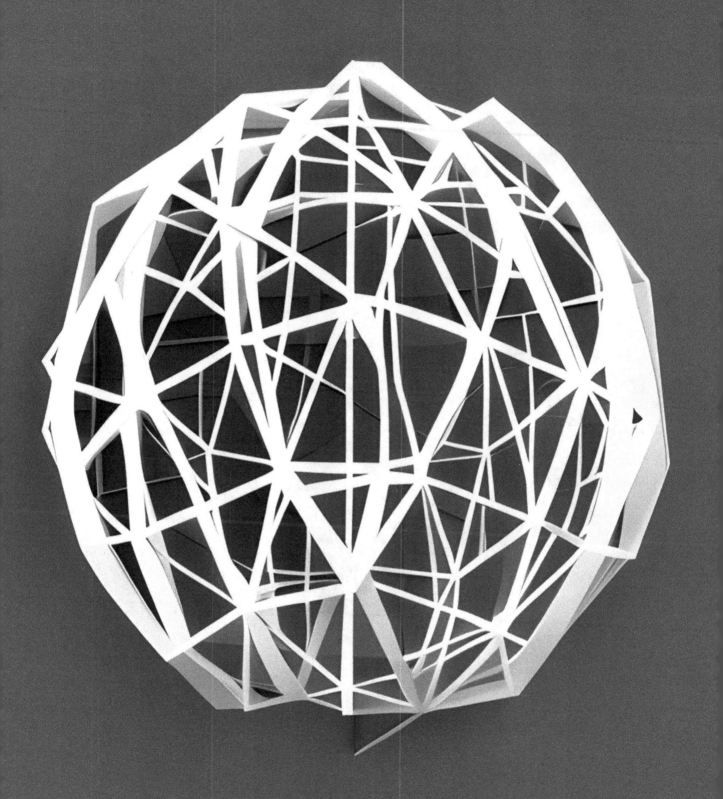

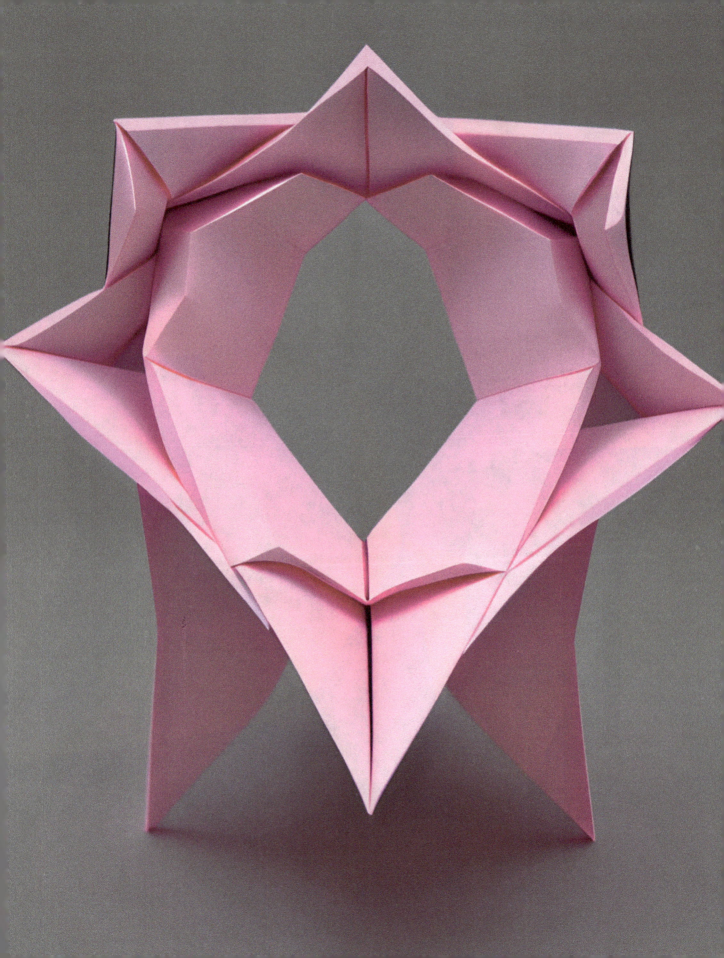

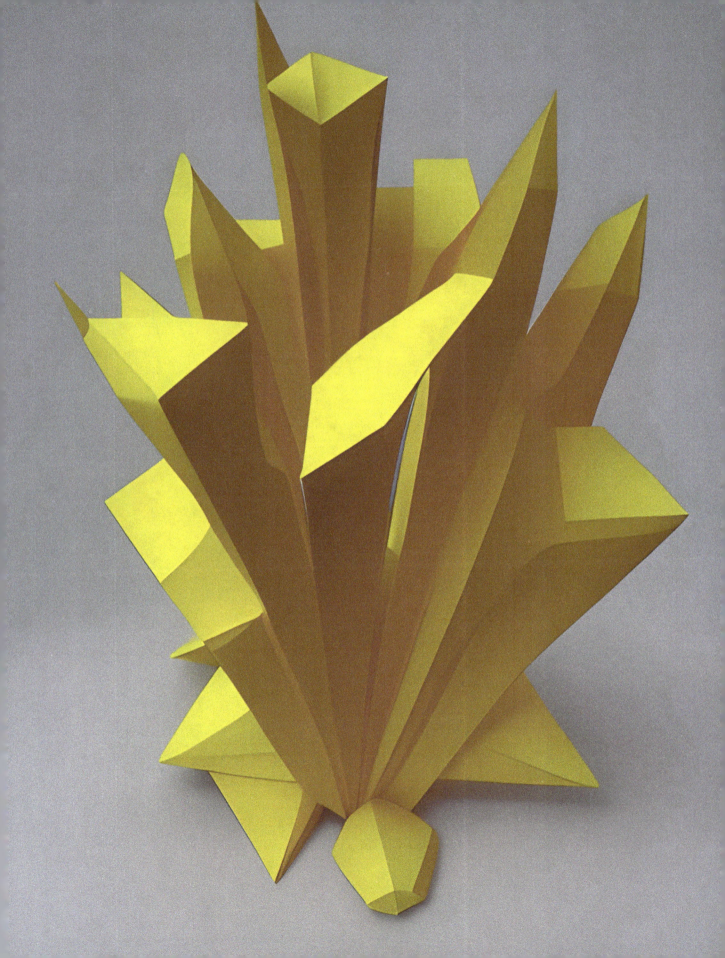

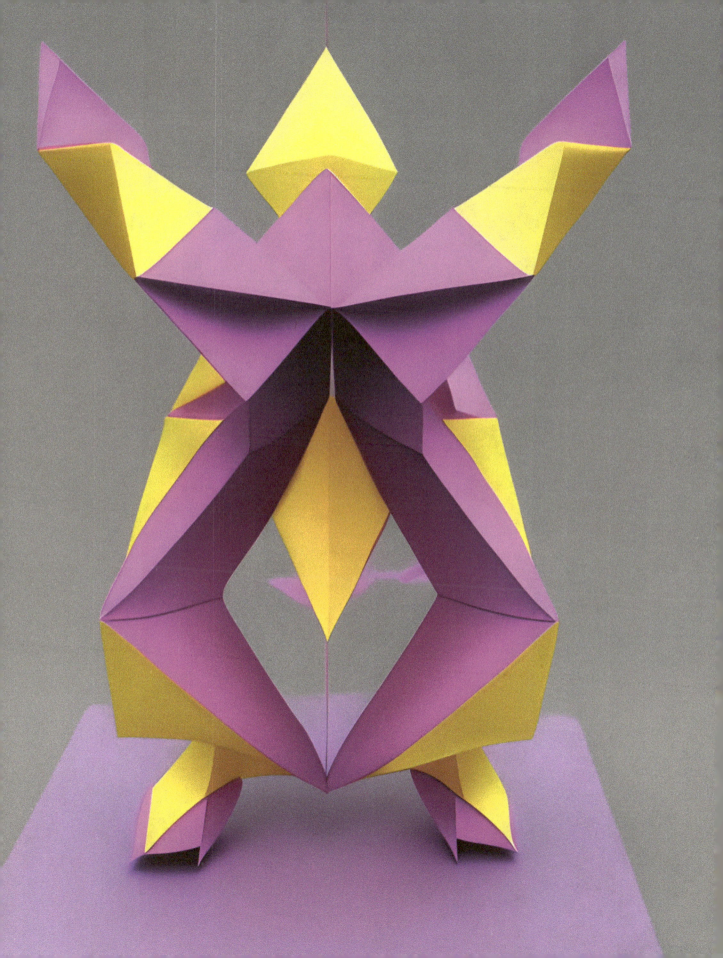

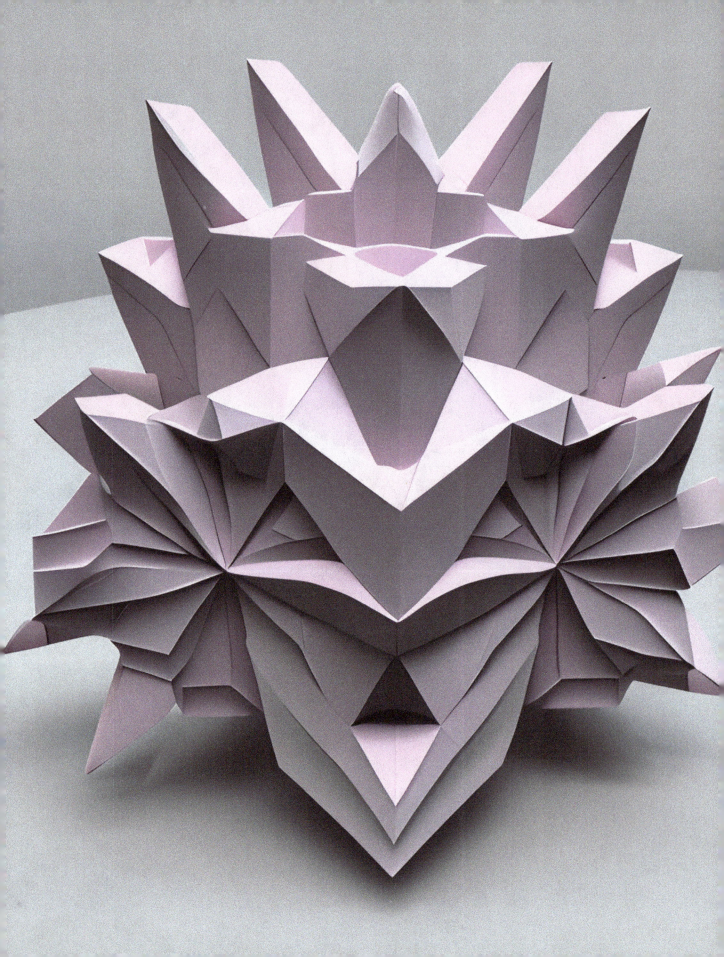

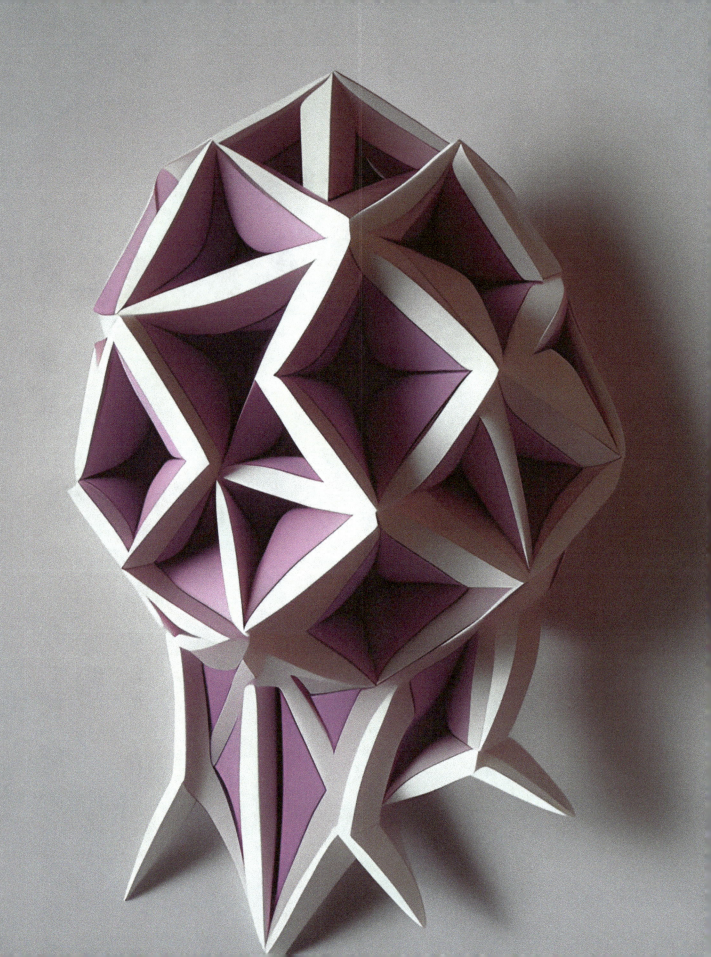

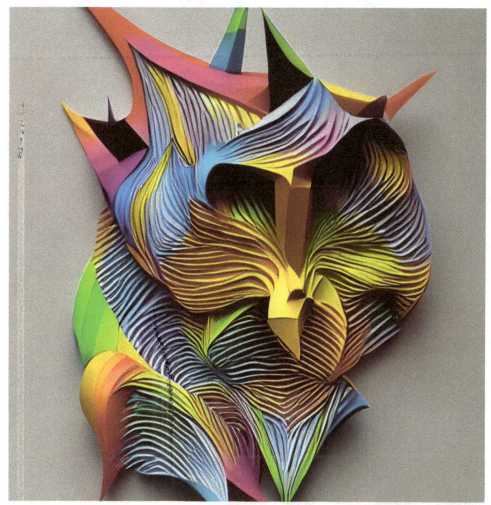

DECOR

72

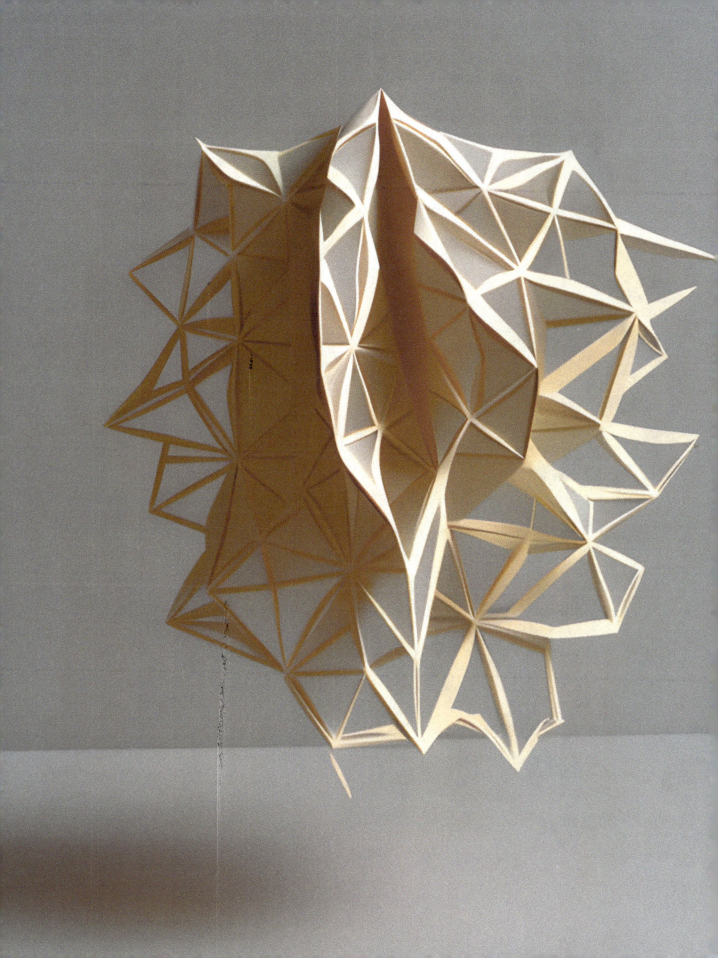

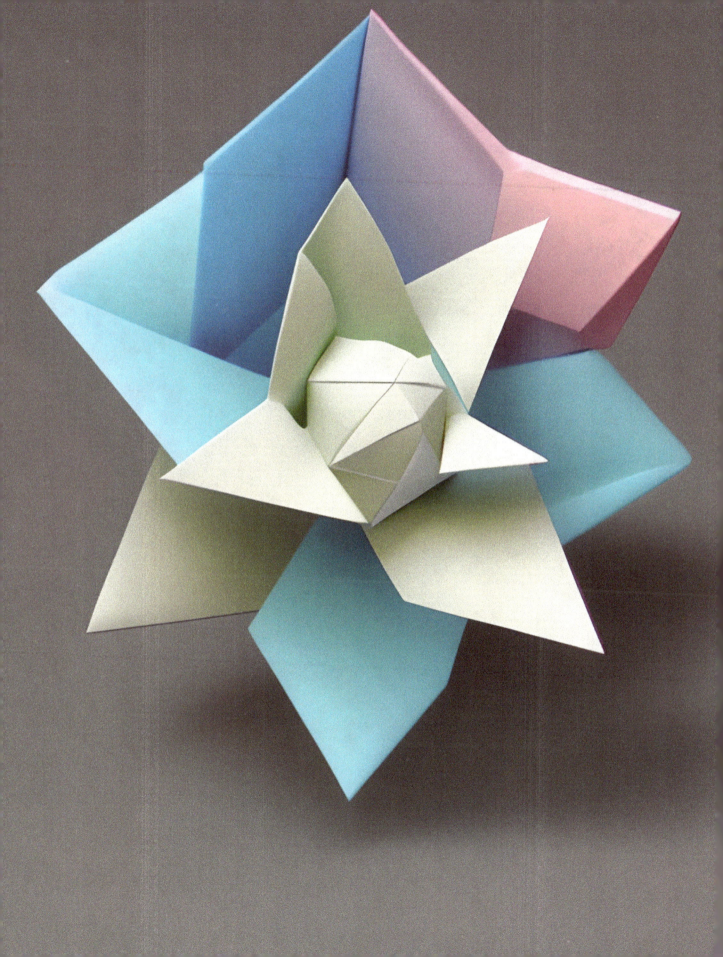

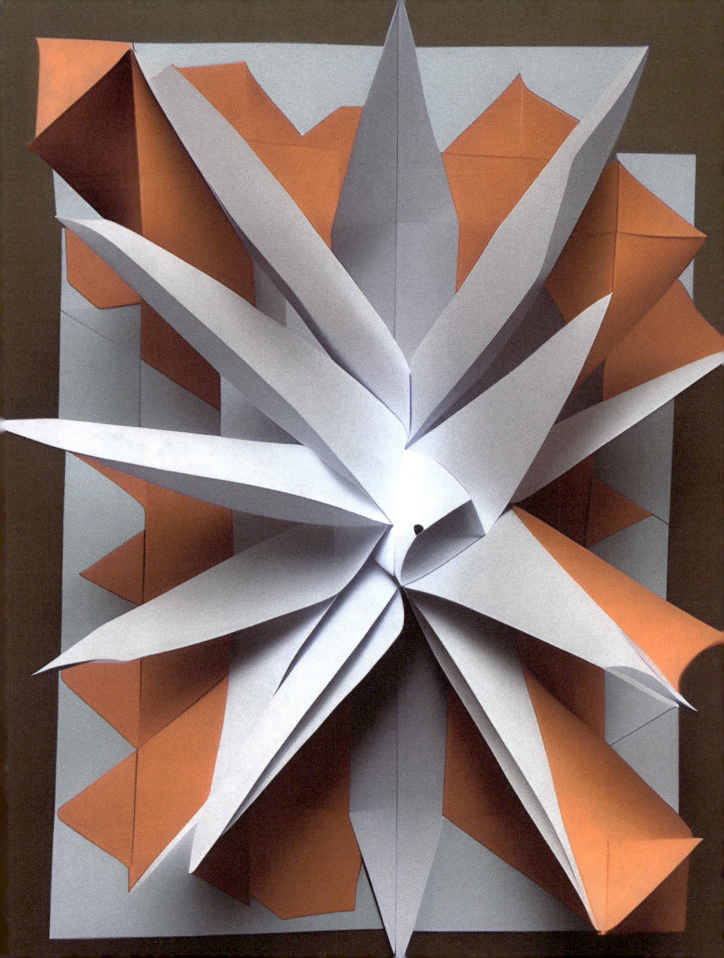

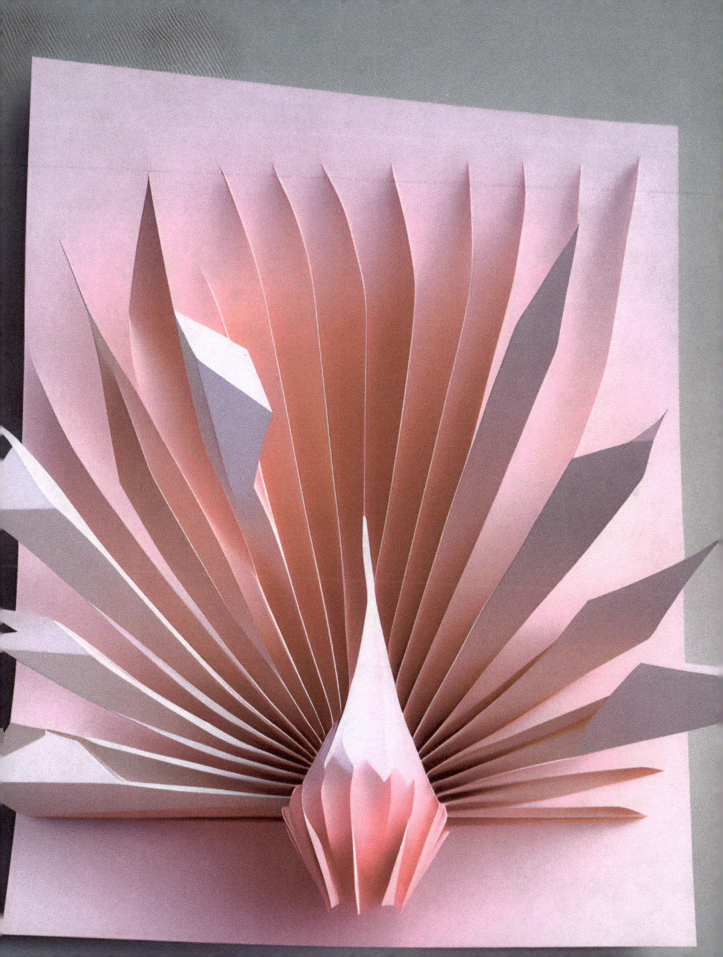

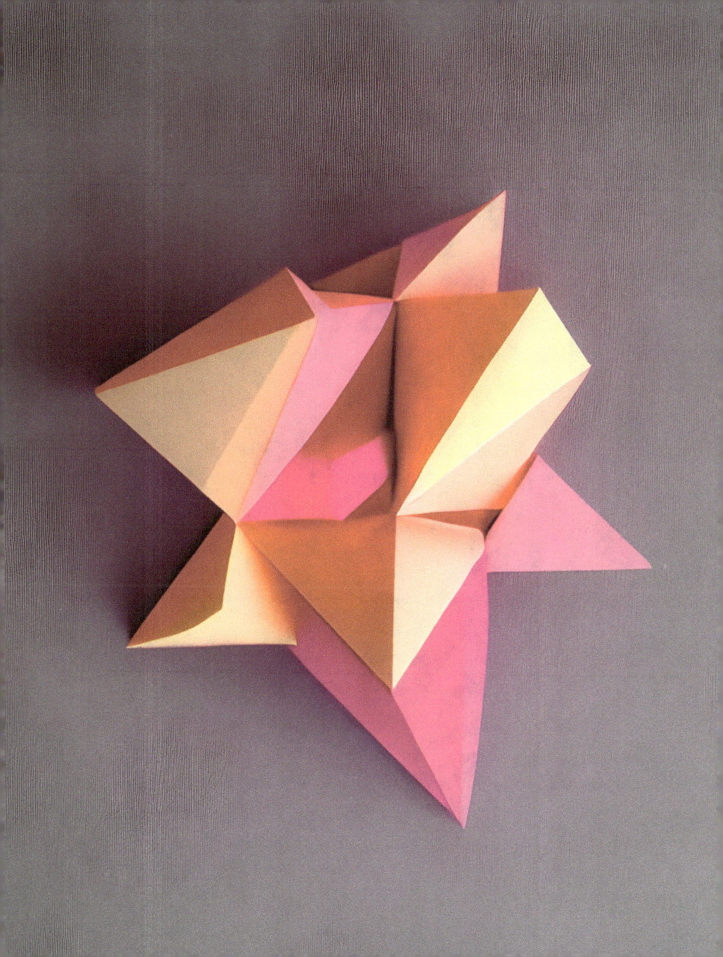

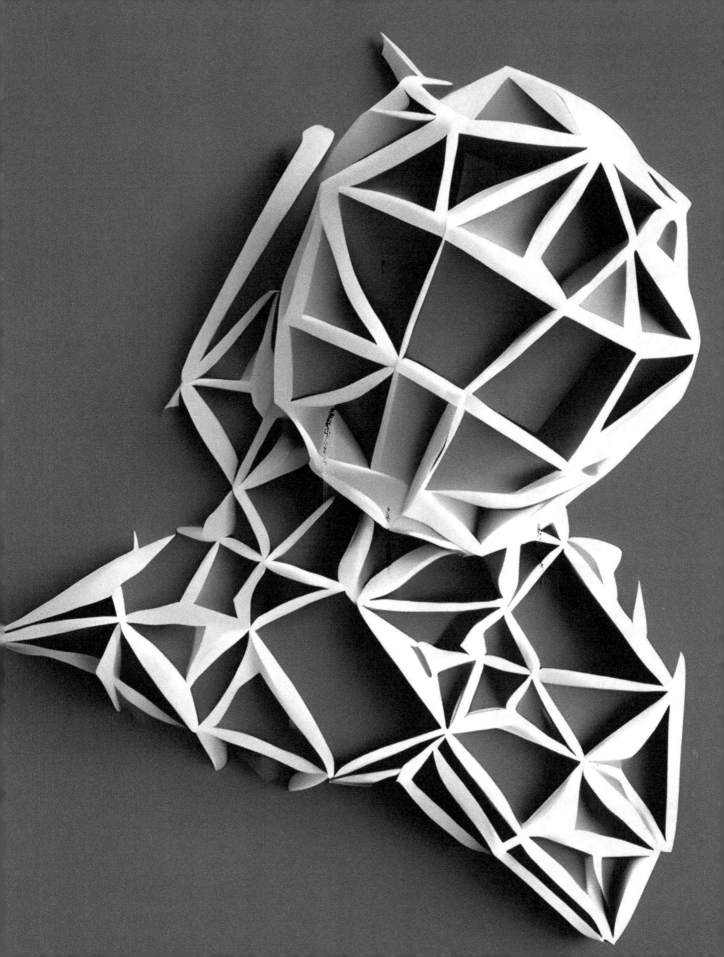

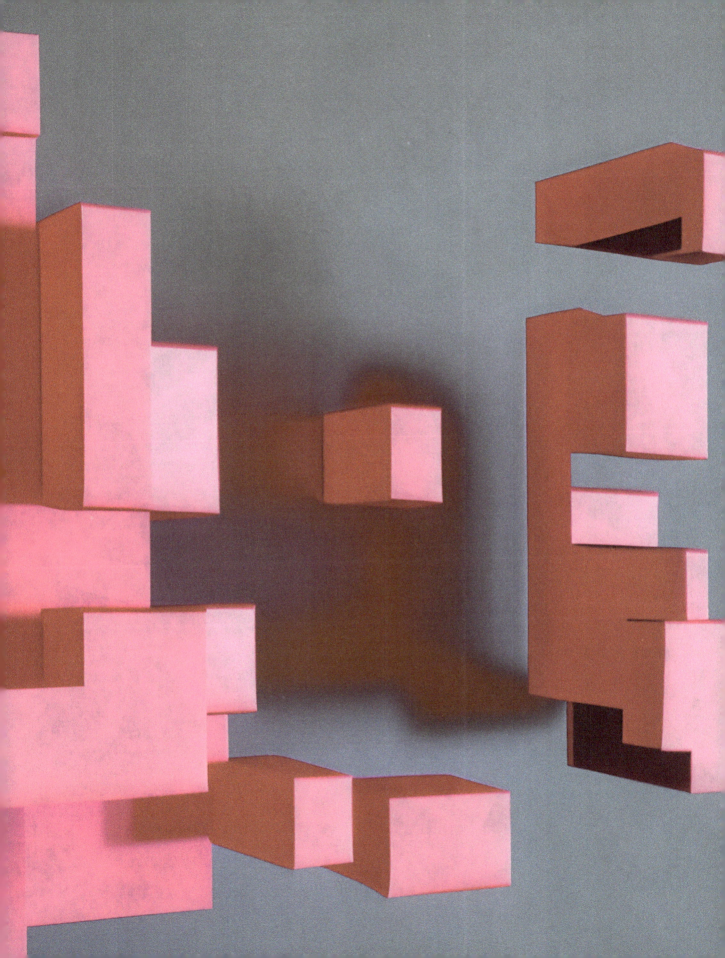

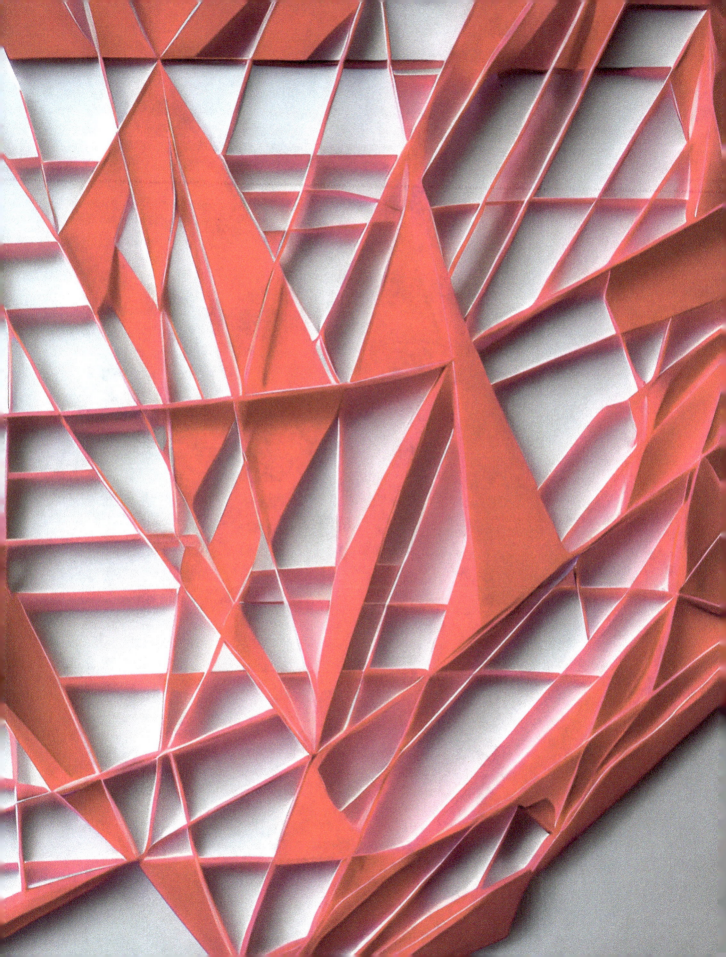

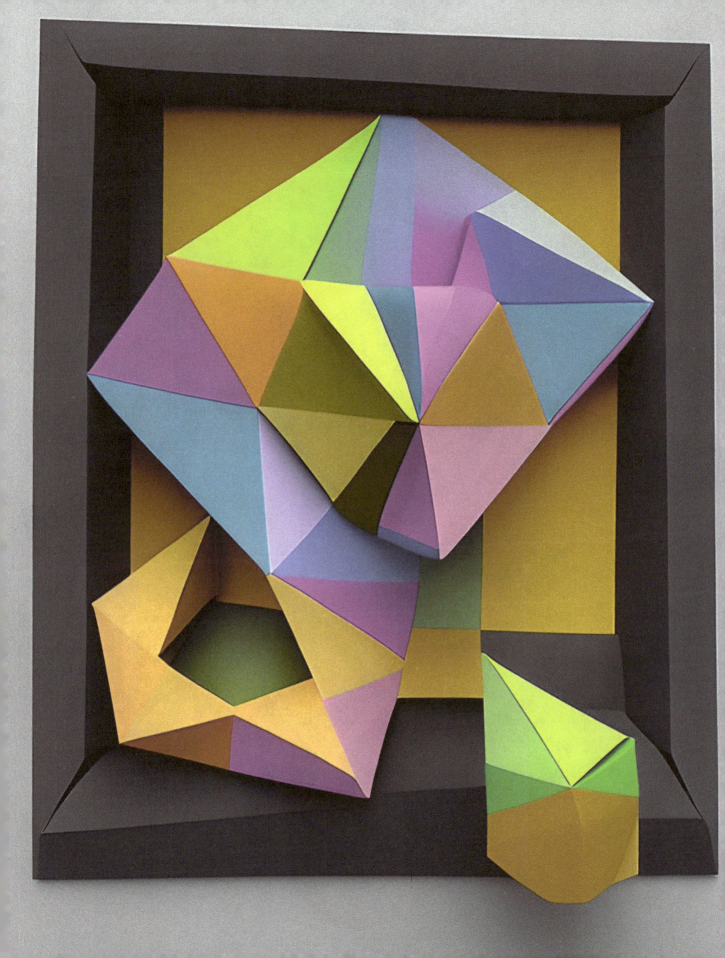

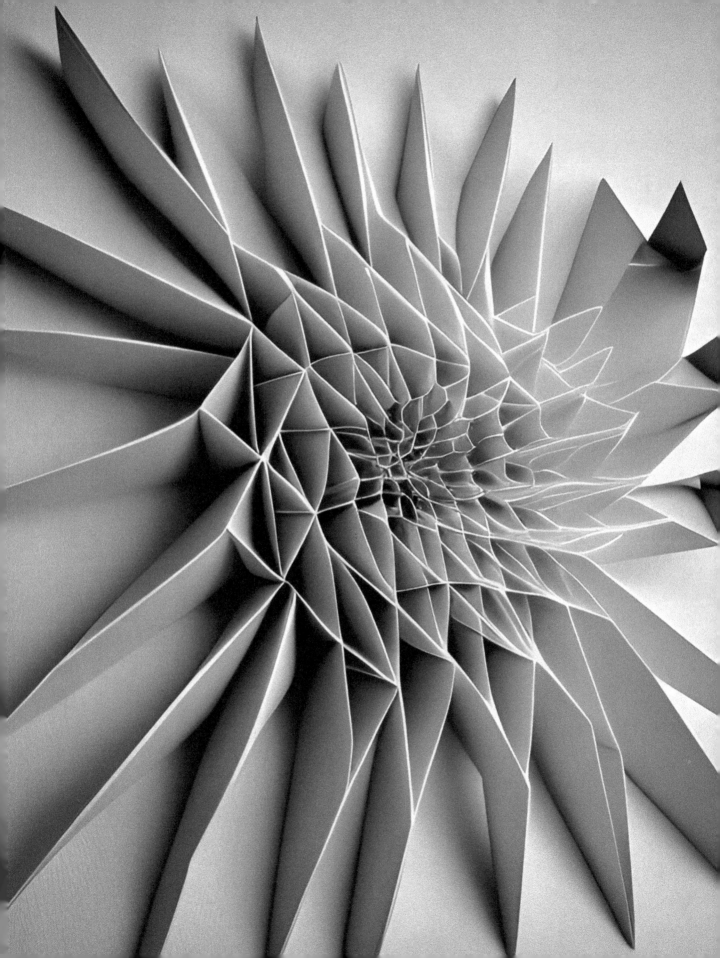

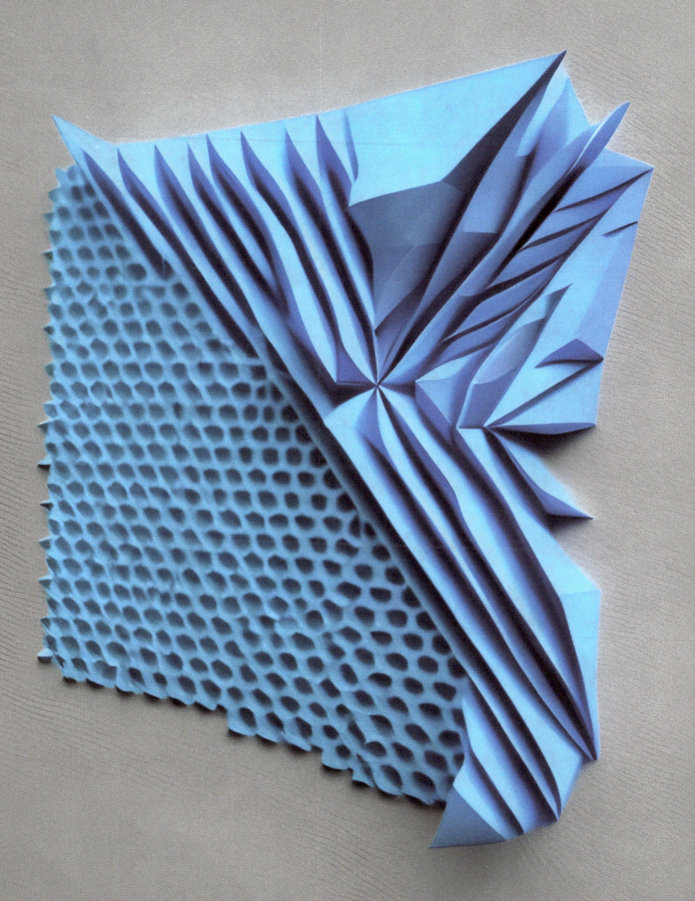

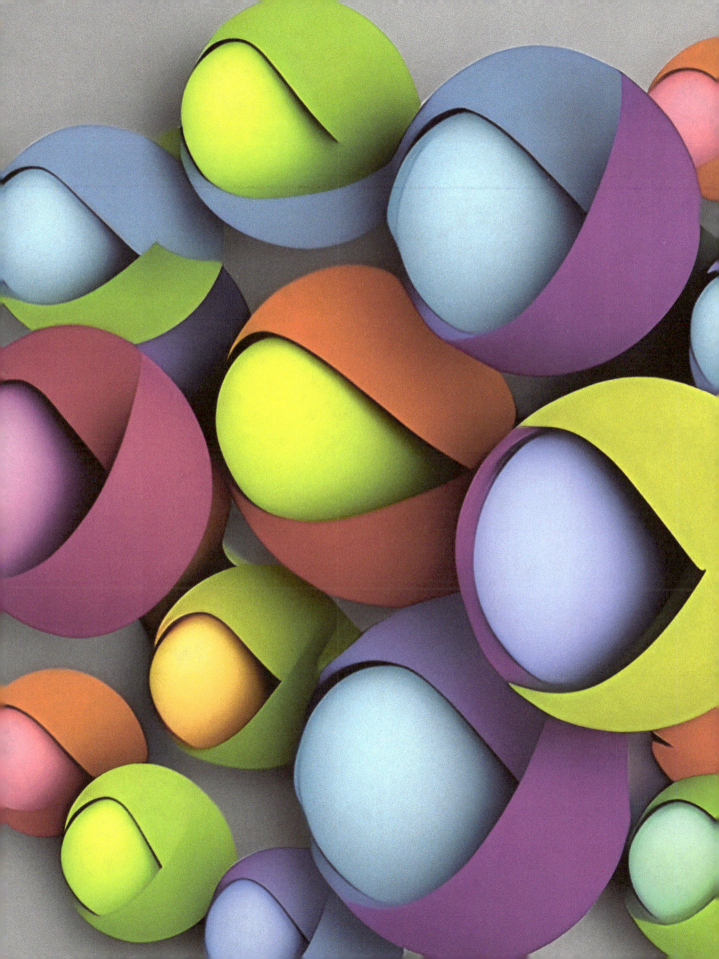

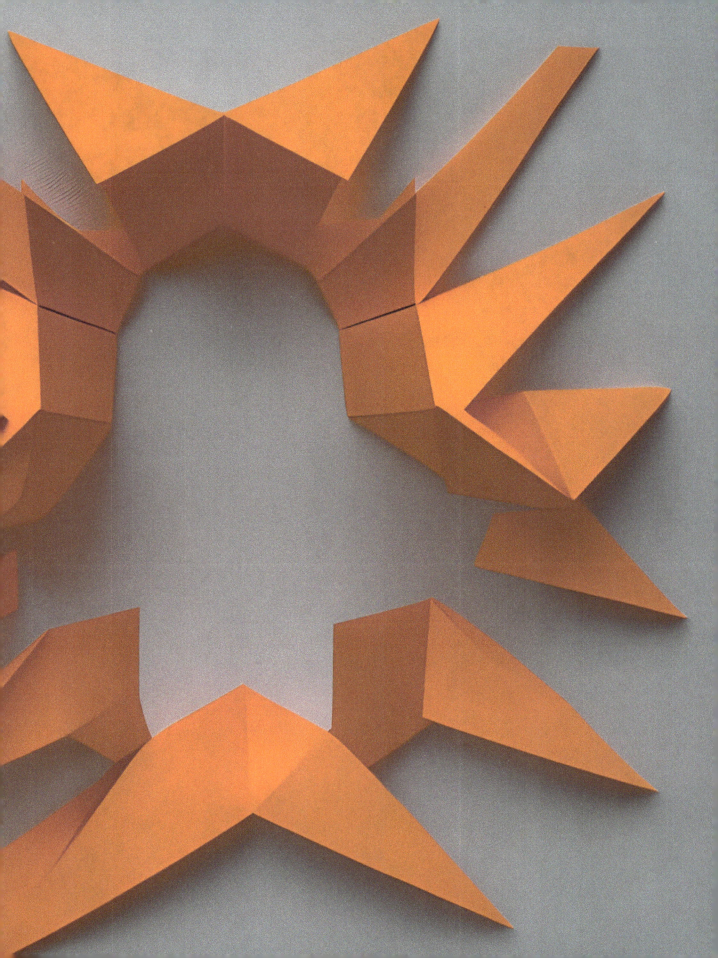

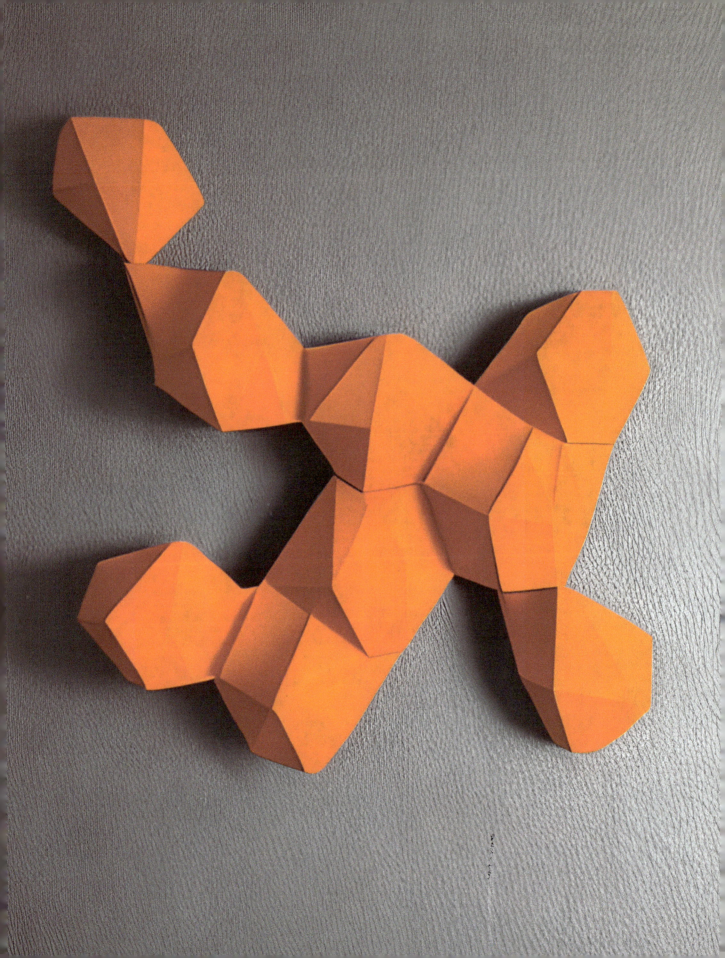

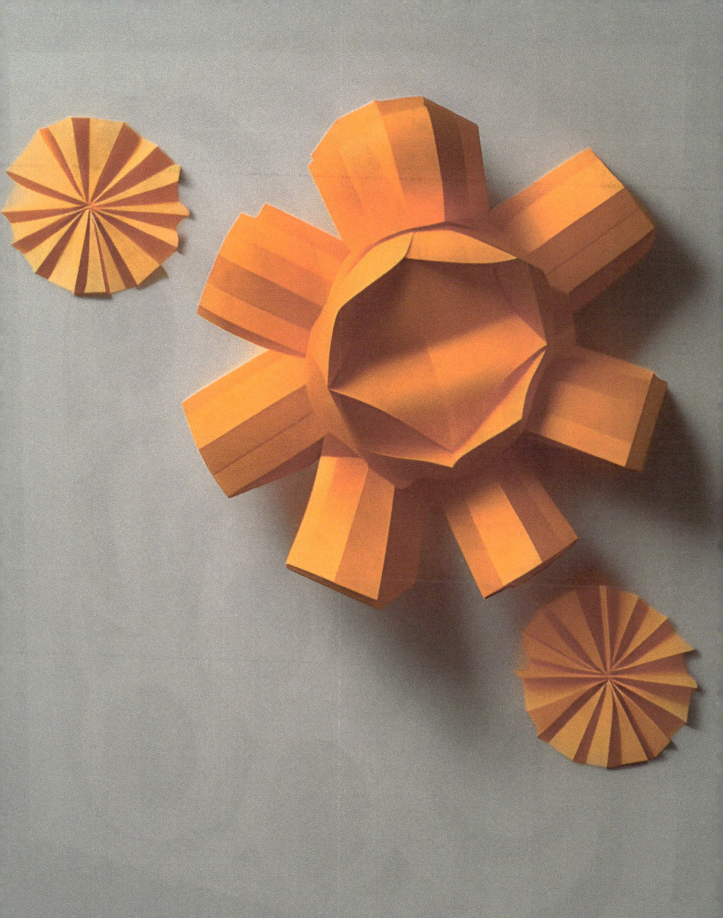

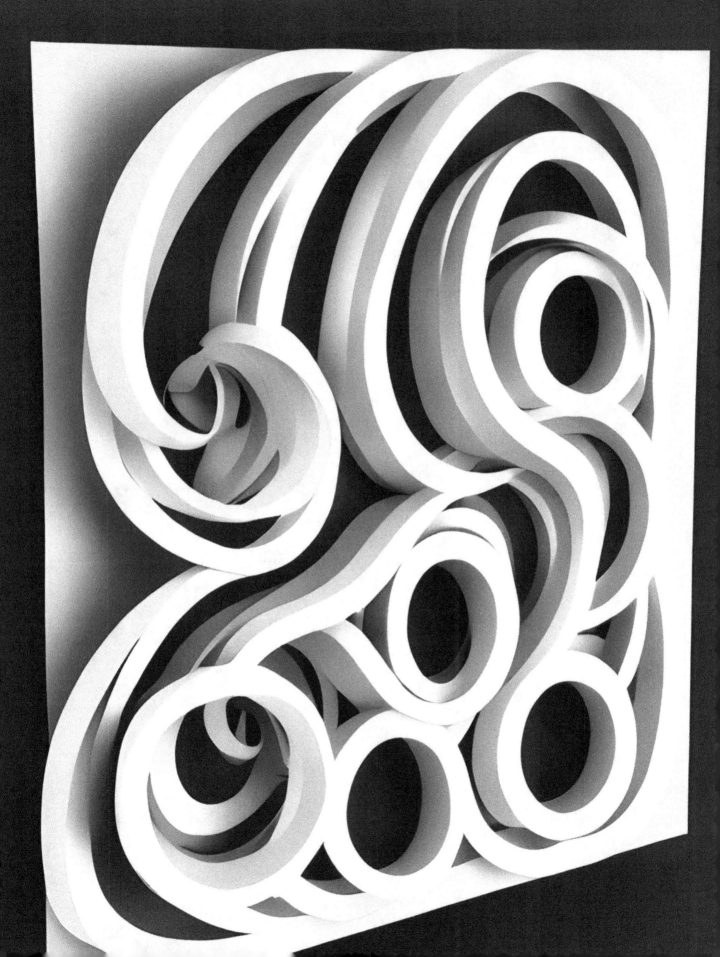

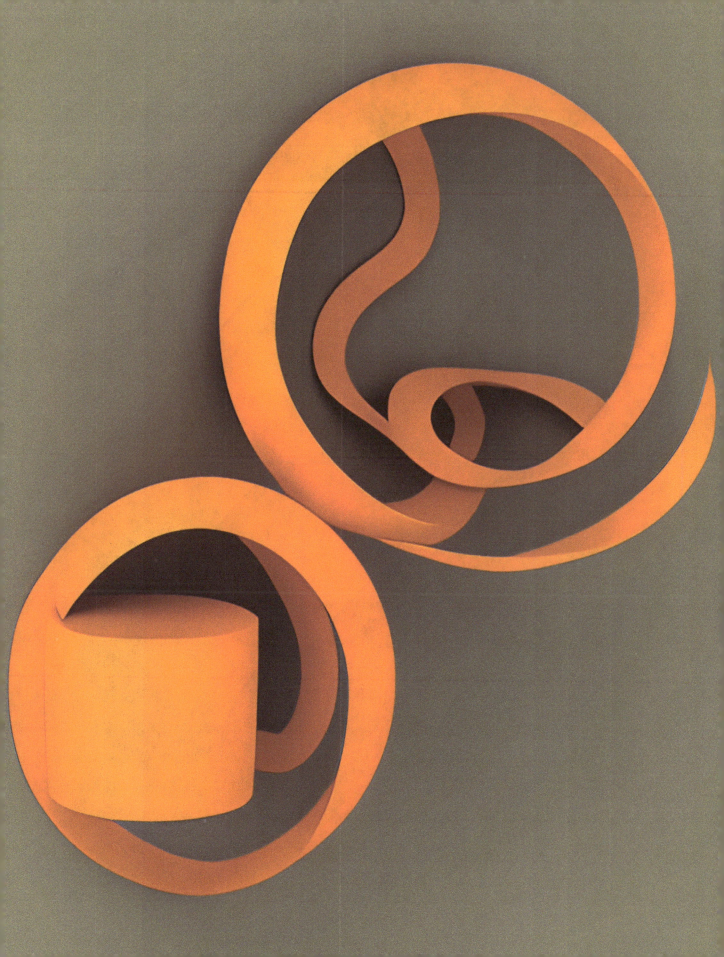

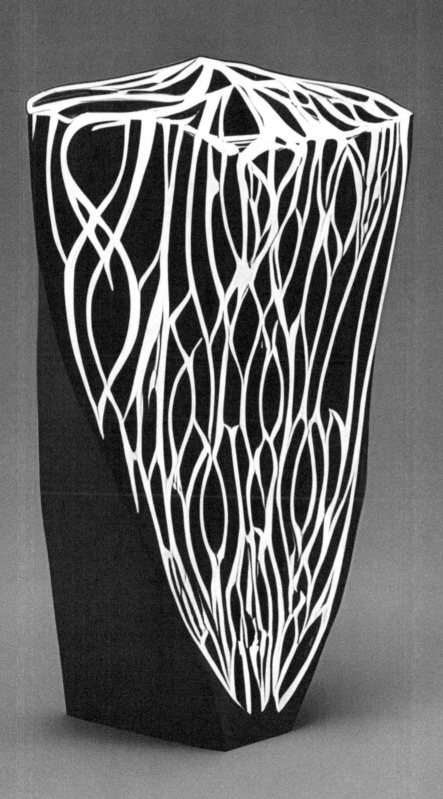

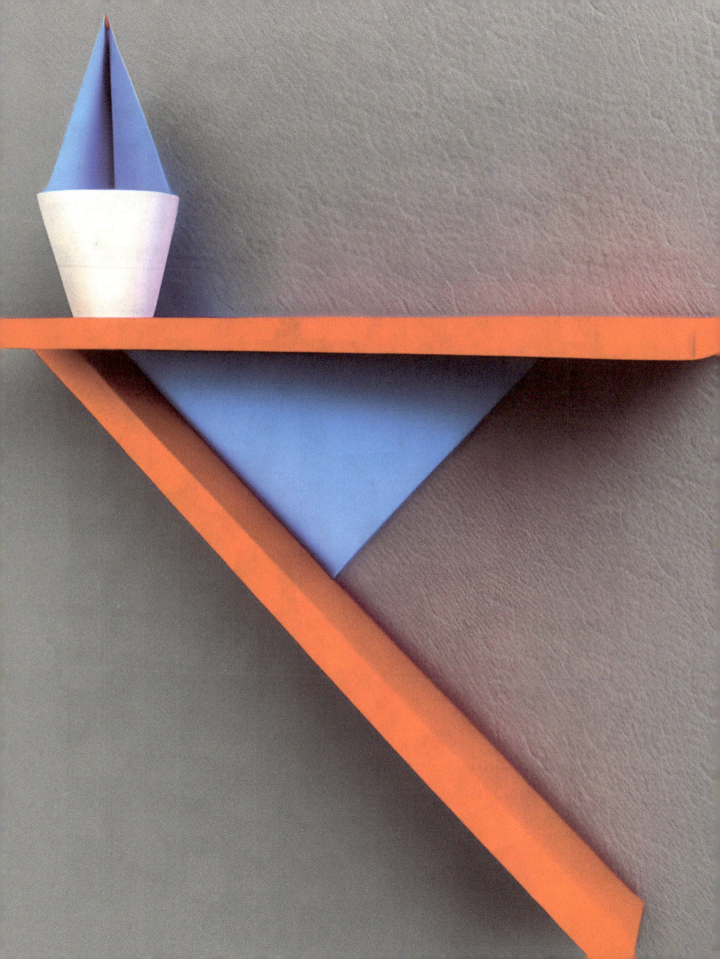

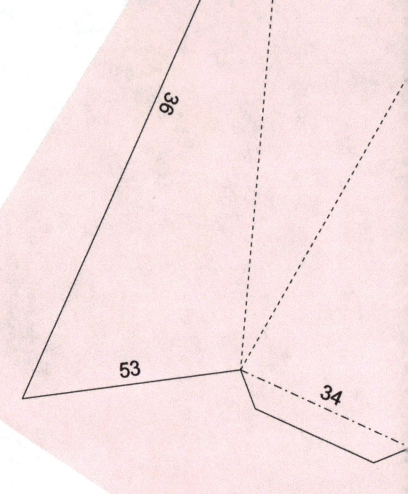

Sofs Designs 2023-24.
First Edition 2023
ISBN 978-0-9865202-9-7
Cataloging data available from
Library and Archive Canada

Look for our other titles:

- 3D papercraft patterns and ideas, Vol 1
- 3D papercraft Inspirations,
  Dragons, Unicorns & Monsters Collection
- 3D papercraft Inspirations,
  Mysticals, Celestials & Robotics Collection

YOUR TURN, SHOW US!

Advancement in Artificial Intelligence (AI) combined human input with the knowledge on how to use this new tool, means we can now provide new never before seen images that will offer makers like you and us innovative inspirations for new paper art projects. **Show us your 3D papercraft inspired art on instagram @sofsdesigns using #sofsinspirations**

32

1